Yuppy Puppy

The Art of Pampering Your Pooch

Yuppy Puppy

The Art of Pampering Your Pooch

BY Binky von Barksdale
Robin Zingone ILLUSTRATOR

BOWTIE
P R E S S

Irvine, California

Karla Austin, Business Operations Manager
Jen Dorsey, Associate Editor, Writer
Michelle Martinez, Editor
Rebekah Bryant, Editorial Assistant, Writer
Ruth Strother, Editor-at-Large
Nick Clemente, Special Consultant
Vicky Vaughn, Book Designer

The dogs in this book are referred to as *he* and *she* in alternating chapters.

Library of Congress Control Number: 2004101936
ISBN 1-931993-47-5

BowTie® Press
A Division of BowTie Inc.
3 Burroughs
Irvine, California 92618

Printed and Bound in Singapore
10 9 8 7 6 5 4 3 2 1

DEDICATION

Sincere thanks to the adorable literati at BowTie Press, especially my typists Rebekah Bryant and Jen Dorsey—your opposable thumbs made it all possible.

This book is lovingly dedicated to every puppy who roams the cold streets without a cashmere scarf; who travels as cargo; and who eats from an unfeeling, plastic, monogramless bowl. My prayers are with you, loves.

—Binky

To all my yuppy puppies—Pepe, Chico, Cha Cha, Quiche, Bosco, Licorice, Jonna, Mandy, Casey, Lenny, Rajah, Rhett, Sheba, Linus, Mona, Murray, Red, Bear, Chita, and Bob.

—Robin

C O N T E N T S

INTRODUCTION

I must admit I was a tad hesitant when my editor approached me to write a guidebook for canines wishing to actively participate in the yuppy puppy lifestyle. A lifestyle is, as those of us in the know *know*, instinctive and not learned. One either drinks bottled or tap. One either watches a rerun of *America's Funniest Animal Videos* or reviews a tape of her performance at last year's Westminster to get tips for the upcoming show season. However, I do recognize the need to aspire to a higher level of living, a more genteel approach to life on four legs. Many of my faithful readers write or send me text messages with questions like, "What's the best way to freshen the highlights in my coat after a day of sailing?"

or "How do I convince my parent to spring for the Volvo wagon instead of the coupe so I can stretch my legs on the drive to the Ethan Allen showroom?" And of course, there is the question that plagues even the yuppiest of puppies, "What's the look this season for rumps with docked tails—stripes or solids?" Pressing matters such as these can leave a canine to wonder whether to hire a lifestyle coach or—*Quelle horreur!*—allow her parent to buy bargain basement chow and give up altogether. Fear not, loves, Auntie Bink is here to guide you. Like a standard poodle making a beeline for the dog salon the weekend before Westminster, I will guide you toward yuppydom like a beacon in the night.

Fashion

A dog's fashion is her personal trademark, so never let her leave the crate without it. A naked dog is, well, a naked dog, and who really wants to look at that? You parents of chubbier breeds especially know what I'm talking about. Here are a few simple rules to always be in style. First, dress your dog for her body type. A corgi should never be seen in horizontal stripes—unless one wants to look like a deranged doormat. Instead, go for classic colors and cuts that enhance her natural beauty. Is she a stick-thin greyhound? Then try a nice, full ball gown for evenings on the town—remember black only accentuates her mile high legs. The stout bulldog should opt for solids, not patterns, to minimize the appearance of butt wrinkles. No matter the breed, always go for classic looks that stand the test of time.

You aren't the only one with light sensitive eyes. Doggles help protect poochie from harmful UV rays.

Going with a trendy look is dangerous, but when in doubt, a cowboy hat and ripped tights are essential for the heroin chic look.

Protect those pads!

Never leave the house without suitable

booties. Summertime demands a versatile

rubber sole for pavement and sand, while

winter is all about traction.

For winter potty times, dress your dog appropriately in thermal wear or polar fleece and the requisite booties.

Acrylic is out! Your dog's leash should only be made of natural fibers—good for the environment and always in style.

Pup Quiz

Your pup's celebrity style is most like:

- Tinkerbell, Paris Hilton's Chihuahua

- Solomon and Sophie, Oprah's cocker spaniels

- Pipi, Sharon Osbourne's Pomeranian

- Bearlie, Justin Timberlake's Yorkshire terrier

Cashmere is the fabric that keeps on giving. No ensemble is complete without a cache muffler, scarf, and sweater. Remember to dry clean only!

When money is tight and

the cashmere has to wait, a

classic cable-knit (in

natural fabric, of course) is

a fashionable alternative.

Who says Halloween is just for kids? A good yuppy puppy embraces the night of the living dead in full regalia whether you choose to dress her as a devil dog or an angel with wings.

Foster your pup's

sense of identity—

monogram everything!

Pup Quiz

Your pup's treasured item of apparel is:

- An elegant Harry Winston leash and collar set

- A stunning Pucci handkerchief to be loosely

  hung from the collar

- An eclectic mix of chunky pearls from

  Chic Doggie by Corey

- A pillbox hat and gloves (classic Jackie O)

Look faboo and help the needy too! Try to buy handcrafted doggy jewelry that benefits a cause.

Do dress for dinner, dahling. Special occasions require special clothing. For ladies, a taffeta ball gown and tiara is appropriate. For gentlemen, a formal four-legged tuxedo is always a smart investment. Remember, tux pants aren't just for formal events. You can dress down your pup by adding a simple shirt and black booties.

Coordination is the key! Matching parent and puppy outfits set you apart from the half-hearted crowd. Although, I do recommend shying away from anything floral, as it only draws attention to a large bustline.

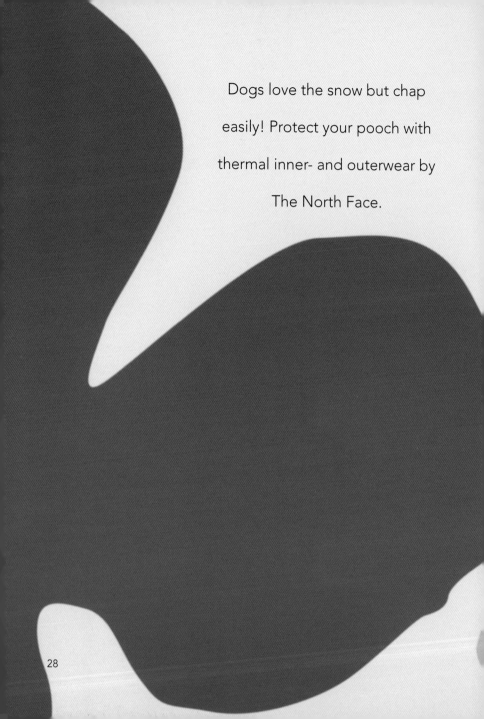

Dogs love the snow but chap easily! Protect your pooch with thermal inner- and outerwear by The North Face.

Purses are the last frontier of fashion. So what if one costs you more than $200? Put your pooch's pic on your purse. It shows you care.

When your dog's style changes or when her Zone Diet starts yielding results, donate used clothes and accessories to the local shelter.

Seek out hotels that provide a complimentary designer raincoat for your pup. After all, there is nothing worse than a soggy dog in a Members Only jacket.

Pup Quiz

Your dog's signature trick is:

- Walking the runway like an '80s Glamazon

- Working the OnStar in your SUV

- Sniffing out better cafés than a Zagat Guide

- Bringing you the lemon zester or garlic press
during time-crunched cooking sessions

Cuisine

A dog's diet is often decided by his human family. It is important to note that this strikes fear in the heart of any self-proclaimed "foodie" dog. Your divine dog may worry about your culinary intentions and fear that you will fulfill his paté needs with bologna. Keep in mind that kibble is an acquired taste and be open-minded to the fact that your pooch may very well exist on a higher culinary plane than other mutts. Be on the lookout for gentle clues that indicate he has a sensitive palate. The sad eye routine works for a lot of my loyal readers, especially during the holidays. Though it doesn't promote good health, he might make a little mess on the floor to indicate his displeasure with the chow du jour. Be perceptive to his dietary needs and choose the most healthful and palate-pleasing meals and treats.

Dry, mealy dog bones are so yesterday.

Try a vegetable-based treat to enhance

antioxidants.

Who knows what evil lurks

in the tap water? Choose

bottled vitamin water to

enhance your pup's diet.

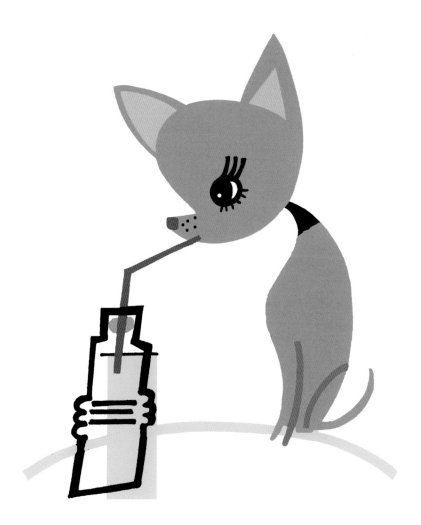

A visit to the local dog bakery is required each and every Saturday. For optimum enjoyment, make sure there is a trendy coffee shop nearby so you can enjoy your treats together.

Pup Quiz

Your puppy recently hosted or was

cordially invited to:

- A Puppy Love Wedding

- A "Bark" mitzvah

- A Leash Release Party

- A Doggy Debutante

It's entirely acceptable

to eat a frozen pizza

so you have more time

to prepare and puree

your dog's

macrobiotic dinner.

Avoid dangerous and unsightly

gristle. Consult your neighborhood

butcher to find out which days he

offers premium beef scraps for sale.

Order from puppy room service

instead of carting your dog's chow

to the hotel room.

Seriously investigate diet options

for your zaftig puppy.

Atkins for dogs, perhaps?

Call the local Williams-Sonoma and inquire about potential availability of Le Creuset dog bowls.

For a fun after work treat,

invite your pooch's friends

over for Yappy Hour

drinks and yappetizers.

Post-holiday switch to weight maintenance chow until your pooch drops the extra pounds.

A tastefully decorated peanut butter and carob cake adds a festive touch to any birthday celebration. However, many pooches over the age of thirty-five in dog years may not appreciate the gesture.

Pup Quiz

Your pup's favorite take out menu is:

• Nobu

• Tommy Bahama's Tropical Café & Emporium

• The French Laundry

• Anything fusion

Invest in a doggy cookbook, preferably

one written by the flavor-of-the-month

chef on Food Network.

Pup Quiz

Your puppy's favorite midnight snack is:

- A bite of whatever you're eating

- Greenies

- Peanut butter cookies dipped in carob

- Leftover foie gras with black mission fig coulis

Make a statement!

Only purchase PETA

recommended chow.

Keep a detailed food journal for

your pooch so you can predict

color and consistency of his

"output" and plan pickup methods

accordingly.

Travel

Dogs love to travel by plane or automobile. Whether it's a day trip to the local farmer's market or tagging along on a safari, always bring your pup along for the ride. Not only does the opportunity to travel expand her cultural horizons, but it also helps her hone vital social skills that can come in handy both at home and in doggy daycare. Fighting the summer crowd in the Hamptons is a fabulous way to foster good will among your fellow well-heeled friends. Holiday should not, however, be purely serious, so be sure to factor in plenty of R&R by scheduling activities such as travel playdates with other hotel guests, doggy massage, and historic walking tours of local dog parks.

No dog is ready for travel without a designer Sherpa carrying case (preferably monogrammed, of course!).

Fly as cargo? Never! The yuppy puppy rarely travels in steerage with the commoners. Who knows what germs she might pick up below the decks?

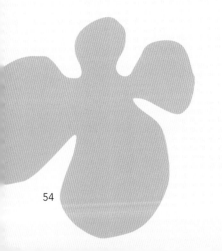

The yuppy puppy's idea of camping is staying in anything less than a four-star property. If, however, nature calls, soften the blow by buying her her own pup tent.

Check out eBay for a
first edition,
autographed copy of
*Travels with Charley:
In Search of America.*

Dogs get thirsty too! A collapsible water bowl is essential whether you are traveling across town or cross-country. While the plastic model is fine for day trips or short walks, employ the stainless steel or mahogany variety for a safari.

Pup Quiz

Your pup won't travel anywhere without her:

- Slobber proof tennis balls

- Doggles

- Goyard Stainless Steel dog bowl carrier

- Monogrammed Sherpa carrying case that fits

  safely under the seat of any domestic or

  international flight.

Ask the concierge if he has a map of area dog parks and fire hydrants. One mustn't stray and accidentally wee in a bad neighborhood.

Pup Quiz

Your dog's dream goal is to be:

- An apprentice under last year's Best in Show at Westminster

- A runway model for the Ralph Lauren Polo pet collection

- Sunning in her own Napa vineyard

- Howling Puccini in Carnegie Hall

Consider using remainder vacation days and travel to Guatemala to drop off donated dog booties.

To assure your dog meets her preferred hotel's weight limit, keep her on a diet and exercise program.

For your pup's safety, clip

her into a doggy seatbelt

harness. Backseat only!

Slip your dog a pre-flight Xanax to ensure a pleasant trip for all aboard.

Consider buying a new car only if it offers the pet package option.

Pup Quiz

Your pup's philanthropic schedule is filled with

activities for which of the following charities:

- SPAY/USA

- Paws to Read

- Guide Dogs for the Blind

- The Delta Society

Every well-traveled pup needs

her own passport.

Grooming and Health

Everyone enjoys the presence of a sharply groomed pup. Neatly arranged fur, a pleasant signature fragrance, and light accessories are sure to get your pup invited into the most prestigious and well-groomed circles. For this reason, it is pertinent that your pup maintains a strict diet and exercise schedule so he looks and feels his best externally and internally at all times. Lengthening off-leash activity sessions and minimizing your pups meals can help him shed the extra pound or two that's been lingering around from all those holiday season scraps and excessive lounging. Keep in mind that "big bones" is not always a positive term, and lethargic equals large with time. It is your responsibility to keep your pup groomed and fit so he can be proud of his appearance.

A fat cat certainly but a
dog never! Help your dog
maintain his target weight
with regulated yogilates
and high protein habits.

Choose your products wisely.

If you are unsure of the best way to

treat your dog's locks, visit a renowned

stylist for a consultation immediately.

Coarse, fine, or frisée fur will

determine your purchasing habits.

When pawlishing toenails avoid

contact with surrounding fur.

The alternative result can be a

shaming and sticky situation

for both you and your pup.

Pup Quiz

Your pup potty trained on:

- The Club Monaco catalog

- *The Wall Street Journal* stock section

- Last year's Williams-Sonoma cookbook

- A faded van Gogh print from that time

  in your life when everything revolved

  around the moods of impressionists

Veer away from generic shampoos. A pup with a wilted mane has cause for becoming a social pariah.

Control shedding by combing your pup daily, follow up with a light massage and a gentle kiss on the paw.

Don't be that yellow fellow. Keep your canine's cuspids clean and bright by brushing with extrawhitening dog paste. For the hopelessly tinged tooth, consider routine laser treatments.

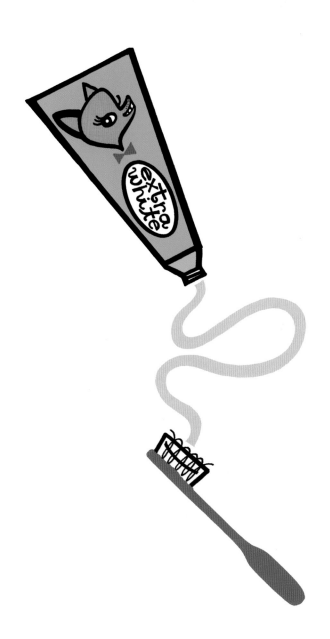

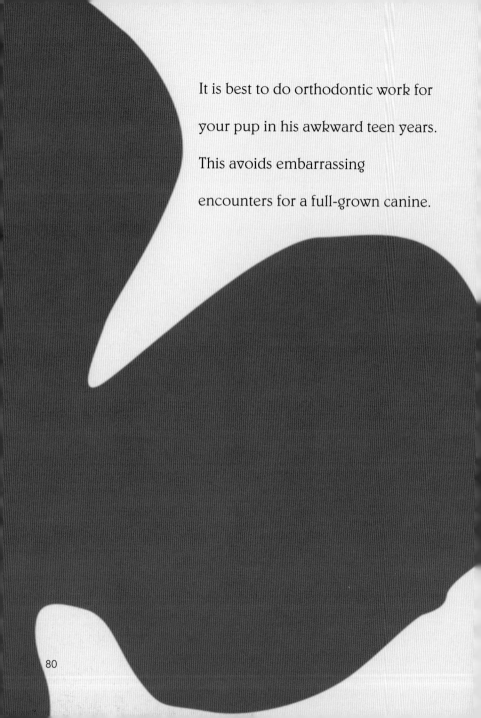

It is best to do orthodontic work for your pup in his awkward teen years. This avoids embarrassing encounters for a full-grown canine.

Refrain from calling your dog's

gathered tufts of fur a pig or

ponytail. It can be unsettling to

be neglected from these socially

accepted terms.

Pierced ears are classy,

but more than two holes

can be ostentatious.

Don't forget your
hydrants. Have your
pup lap up at least
eight bowls of water a
day for a sheen coat
and shiny nose.

A hose bath is an insufficient

method of cleansing. Period.

Pup Quiz

If your pup misbehaves you consider:

• Adoption counseling

• Pet psychology (Not psychiatry—you
don't believe in treating any ailments
with unnatural drugs)

• Tough love

• No snickerpoodles for a week

Your pup's signature scent is best

developed by multiple applications of

aromatherapeutic spritzers.

For pups with wanderlust it is crucial to

strictly avoid carbohydrates in the evening.

Most hotels only accept dogs of a svelte

physique—fewer than twenty-five pounds.

Never underestimate the power of an invigorating run through an open field or a refreshing loofah through one's midsection.

Pup Quiz

You have improved communication with

your dog by:

- Investing in the Bow-Lingual

- Visiting a pet psychic

- Making sure your pup's e-mail inbox is full

- Leaving your pup homemade greeting cards

to thank him for the "little things"

Wipe, wipe, wipe—no one

enjoys a leaky orifice.

For a French breed a
French manicure is
fitting, for other
breeds—pawlish to
the occasion.

Do your part by picking up

after your pup. Scented and

color coordinated Wag Bags

are now available for a stylish

and efficient cleanup.

Decorating

Being in the doghouse does not have to connote negative feelings any longer. In fact, a pup's abode should be equal in comfort to your own. Your pup's style and personality is the perfect way to hone in on the difficult decisions that come along with doggy decor. If your pup is active, photographs of her mountainous or beach-roaming adventures will work well as a collage on a French memo board hanging above her alcove. If she is more of a homebody, a cozy lounging area filled with her favorite throws, overstuffed floor pillows, and an organized cabinet of toys and treats may be the better way to decorate. Whatever your pup's disposition make sure to incorporate it throughout your home and adjoin both of your themes in a cohesive and classic manner.

A pup's room should be the reflection of her soul. Try not to create an area that may conflict with your dog's zeitgeist.

A hand-painted dog dish (when glazed properly) can be just the right accent to dark wood flooring, slate, or travertine.

A dog's resting quarters should be inviting. Sleigh or canopy beds provide your pup with a minivacation from this dog-eat-dog world.

Linoleum, garage-slicked-cement, and artificial turf should never come into direct contact with your pup's fur during rest times.

When arranging mason or cookie jars of homemade dog treats remember the cardinal rule of clusters, "Odds are in, evens are out."

Pup Quiz

Your dog's middle name is:

- Van der

- Saint

- de la

- of (followed by a remote location in Wales)

Oversized floor pillows for your

pup should head the minimum

300-thread count.

It's about time quality and cozy are combined. Start a Frette for Pet petition. Demand that the line be created and sold at fine boutiques near you.

A clear Lucite or metal handled scoop is an attractive way to dish your doggy her delights and avoid messy spillage.

Accessories and toys should be neatly tucked away in their own storage chest or closet area. Custom pewter hooks are great pieces to hang leashes, treats, umbrellas, and Wag Bags in an organized and easily accessible arrangement.

Pup Quiz

Your dog's favorite movie is:

- *My Best Friend's Shedding*: A quirky comedy where all hair breaks loose!

- *Reservoir Dogs*: Another Rin Tin Tarentino masterpiece!

- *You've Got Tail*: A remake of the famous *Piddle Stop Around the Corner*!

- *Who's Afraid of Virginia Wolfhound*: The acting alone deserves a round of appaws.

When considering portraiture of your pup, oils tend to be a safe traditional medium. For a more modern look screen-printed Warhols have enthusiastic panache.

Place strong classic dog titles such as *The Call of the Wild*, *Travels with Charley: In Search of America*, and *The Hound of the Baskervilles* throughout your dog's living quarters for a well-rounded erudite feel. Note: *Old Yeller* is taboo for obvious reasons.

Don't be antisocial! Place a welcome mat, doorbell, and other inviting exterior decor in front of your pup's doggy door. These accessories provide curb appeal and a warm reception foyer for neighborhood pups.

Fabric swatches are a handy way to match the hue of your dog's fur to your custom valences or plantation shutters.

Be proud of your pup's accomplishments. A framed AKC registration should be hung adjacent to all higher education diplomas.

Pup Quiz

Your dog's favorite front seat is:

• The 'Vette (leather interior, dual climate

control, and seat heaters)

• The Ford Focus (who can get enough

of the pet package?)

• The Range Rover (an SUV with a

classic moniker)

• The Jag (she loves to take this cat for a ride!)

When choosing a home, be sure that your zip code is zoned for the best of doggy daycares or at least cast your ballot for training school vouchers.

Wegman pieces are passé, but sharp, unusually cropped black and white dog photography can add a necessary punch to an otherwise bland room.